MOTHER-
GHOSTS

Leah Sewell

Woodley Press
Washburn University
Topeka, Kansas

Several poems in this collection have been published in the following journals and anthologies: *To the Stars Through Difficulties: A Kansas Renga, Blue Island Review, 150 Kansas Poems, Coal City Review, Midwestern Gothic, Stone Highway Review, Roufus City Review, Bear Review, Spry* and *[PANK]*. "The Crimson Lady" was nominated for the Pushcart Prize. Some of these poems appeared in the chapbook *Birth in Storm* (2012), ELJ Press, and Coconut Books broadsides (2014).

For Ashley, for the Topeka Writers Workshop,
for Sylvia and Oliver.

Contents

Introduction

I first became aware of Leah Sewell's poetry at a reading. I didn't know her at the time. There were others reading that afternoon as well and already I'd begun looking at the clock, my mind drifting long before she took her place behind the microphone. But from the first few lines, I found myself sitting up straighter, listening with intensity. It struck me how intuitively she understood the ways in which lyric and narrative can coalesce to create poems that are both clear and numinous. The narrative qualities don't veer into the anecdotal and her lyric impulses don't consume meaning. And because of this, what we receive from the work are revelations of experiences related to childhood, adolescence, young adulthood and motherhood that recount the universal emotional qualities associated therein, but are also more fully illuminated through the unique sensibility of the poet/speaker.

Of course, that's the goal of all poetry, isn't it? But Leah, more than most poets, takes the familiar and through her penetrating gaze regenerates that which we mistakenly believed we wholly understood. The poems, distinctive in their diction, full of beautifully compressed images and authenticity of voice, provoke a response much like mine that afternoon—immediate and potent.

Could there be a more apt title for this collection than *Mother-Ghosts?* If so, I can't imagine what that is. Specters and visitants permeate the collection as does the vast realm of what it means to mother or be a mother. The voices of Annie Oakley, Baba Yaga and Belle Starr are heard in this collection (among others) and their significance is felt individually, but are made even more powerful by their juxtaposition with the other poems. Their disembodied voices no more haunting than the speaker's as she recounts the journey from innocence to experience, revealing how too quickly and too soon the two can be intertwined.

If I seem to be speaking a great deal about dichotomies, it's because the work and Leah's voice elicits such a response in me. Fear and desire, resistance and resignation, the difficult disparities between hopes and realities abound. She recognizes the inscrutable mystery of love— how easily it can range between comfort and distress. But she doesn't impose these contrasts onto the work, they rise naturally from a clear-eyed poet who has the ability to truly see the world, who understands the complexities of relationships and connectedness and gains strength through those divisions.

But here's what I appreciate most about this book and what struck me page after page after page after page: *Mother-Ghosts* reveals Leah's gift with the lyric and proves that the narrative form can still surprise.

- Teri Youmans Grimm, author of *Dirt Eaters* and *Becoming Lyla Dore*

Mother-

Ghosts

Alfalfa Child

my second summer I learn
to run naked in the fields

gumming wet leaves
cling to my burst skin

morning sky a sheet
where spilled juice climbs

see power beyond pull of milk
reel away from Mama's blouse

whole lit plain tilting
toward me bottomless chasm

till breathless she rustles behind
little nightgown held in her fist

Farm Kids at Town School

Kelly at the next desk
wears his dad's pig farm
in his shirt.

Brianna is thin
shins in galoshes.
She smells
like Carmex,
shivers in the creaking
farm house
three fields down.
Her big dad
throws wood
in a basement stove.
Sounds like a monster
belching fire
down below
sleepovers.

I forget to wear socks
but Mom's too busy
feeding flapjacks
to Dad's canyon hunger
to notice.

Kelly gave me his heart
on Valentine's,
slid it in my locker.
He knows and I know
but we never say.
At home it sits
with dead flies
on my windowsill.
Kelly smells of pigs.

Broken Ulna

In the day while Mother sleeps, I tiptoe
into her room and unscrew the caps of her creams.
The Egyptian woman on the Oil of Olay label
is nothing like Mother with her perm
and new cigarette habit, her scarred cheeks
smiling after three or four drinks.

I jump off the top bunk. I think I can fly,
palpable weight in the air of home will
hold me aloft. Ulna juts through skin like a finger
turning off my light switch. Stars settle
on my eyelids. I have made trouble

in my demand for care. Stretched on the sofa,
arm locked in cast and sling, I suck on a penny
while Mother vacuums the hazy room.
The copper clot lodges in my throat. I can't

breathe. I writhe and flail mending limb at Mother
in her cloud of dust and noise. The ledge of coin
winnows into my red insides, scrapes a path. Heavy
        in my belly, it sits,
the secret. The weapon.

Sister

On her bed, she petted
the white kitten with fleas and sharp
shoulder blades, its mother missing since the tornado.
The stereo played White Snake. A coiled rubber
lay next to a bowl of candy
strawberries on the night table. A box fan
whirred humidity into
the long hair of a sleeping boy on her floor,
his red ear swollen from safety pin piercing,
and swayed the chain lock
she bought from the walking distance store
and yard work allowance.
Get out, she hissed. Her room
smelled like old blood, like bathroom trash.

I saw her behind Century Mart, a dark
wooded place with burnt stone buildings
and trees skinny as cats. She swung
low under clawing branches,
threaded down to the place where river
smells like dead fish and mildew mattresses
stick out like sick tongues from the bank's caves.

I packed my shoplifted cigarettes,
returned home where Mother was idling at the curb
on her way off to museum night guard shift.

By dusk, slow dark swallowed
me and the house. The sirens sounded,
second time since Tuesday, trees knocked
on the door, phone trilled long on the wall.

In Rock County, a fifteen-year-old girl
bled to death, her cause
unknown, her hand resting in the river
where it foamed like a sick mouth.
A boy cried many tears into his long hair,
and a white kitten mewled so incessantly
I had to put it out, tornado or not,
set it to fend like its long lost mother.

Dark Wisconsin

The first winter I live with
Aunt June in Madison, God
docks his dark ship over
the schoolyard. I go pale.

Afternoons, I wait
on the window seat for my mother
to stand from the wreckage, make
her way down Bonner Lane
in scuffed Keds, press
the chime doorbell, take me home.

Each evening when the light
shifts from gray to cobalt,
Uncle Jeff comes in
stomping snow, fills the bathroom
with Old Spice steam. I sleep

in the sewing room with
a life-sized doll in the closet
keeping watch and the mean
cat curled in the corner. On weekends,

Uncle Jeff tickles me until I cry
real tears and Aunt June appears
in the doorway saying *stop.* Sundays
are tights, church, and ladies
snipping coupons in the kitchen,
laughing through their noses.
Uncle Jeff struts in, wearing only
his Velcro towel fastened
at hairy waist, dribbles
coffee into catchphrase mug
till the ladies howl and

Aunt June's mouth tightens.
Mother never comes. Sometimes
I grimace so hard my chapped cheeks
break open. I lock eyes with the cat
until his amber globes glow like planets
and I know he longs to be wild,
sun warming the body and
everywhere to go.

mom,

i love you even though you are dead i would tell you to your face
will you show me your face i won't be scared
you can see mine it is bigger tell aunt june
my teeth are straight enough i won't need braces
i am not glad you burned up but a little glad you know
if you can read my thoughts
because that song about your body when you die
(don't ever laugh when a herse goes by)
and you didn't have to be worm food after all so that's some thing
i didn't see you die so i don't really believe it
did you make it up are you on vacation you know me
i believe any thing but every one cried even
me (alot) and are you really gone you're like that joke about laps
the part of the body you lose when you stand up

After Death: Annie Oakley Appraises Herself in the Mirror

My rifles are limbs I lift now and admire.
Frank stands behind me gesturing a pistol. I never feared
bullets. Not once was I shot, although during love
I imagined my veins burst like glass balls filled of red powder.

My corset no longer pinches because I no longer
breathe. Medals pinned to my chest flap like butterflies
when someone visits. Buffalo Bill comes, Edison,
sad drunk Calamity, cobwebbed Queen Victoria,
Dave, our sweet pooch, trotting around with an apple
perched between his ears. Even old Sitting Bull wanders
into my dressing room on occasion, appears confused,

and in his wake—hare, deer, squirrel I'd like Mother to sear
and stew, but I believe she's detained
in Darke County woods considering signs that point
in three directions to her husbands. Besides,
I am no longer hungry. Yet my cheeks seem gaunt, receding.

I kiss the barrels and blow smoke onto the mirror glass.
You're the star, Frank says, twirls his gun, winks
at my reflected gaze. Yes, he's right. I've still got it.

The Crimson Lady

Weirder, still, is the tale
of red-tipped leaves in the field
behind Aunt Patty's trailer
in Romeo, a bruised kind of town
in Michigan, famous for its peaches.

They say that a man not unlike
Uncle Paul with pokey mustache
and caterpillar eyebrows that dive
quick into lightning bolts

lost his mind over his wife,
chased her down
with a hacksaw
and got her
in the field before

the dry creek that if you follow
leads out to the Frosty-Freeze.

She probably deserved it.

My cousins swear
on blood-soaked earth,
point to the plants' red tips—evidence.

The killer probably wore his work boots,
dirt-brown with lolling tongues like Uncle Paul's,
and she barefoot from doing dishes
or maybe in house slippers only.

Aunt Patty never even leaves,
only cranks the window
for a cigarette. She might not even own
a lousy pair of shoes.

Thirteen Tastes like the Pantry Floor

and the bottom of the hamper—forgotten blood and taffy, tastes like edible cellophane, like gnawing on lacquered bunk bed post, till initials of your teeth reach pulp. Tastes like thieved quarters, forgotten blood, plaque, bus exhaust, cab exhaust, boys' pointy tongues. Changes with seasons: frozen pine needles disguise tobacco, peppermint Nair scalds legs—clean slates for sun to stroke. You suck on your Kool-Aid hair, it freezes into a knife. You chip rough bark, bite your fingernails, eat like a starving doe. The taste of new grass you claw up like a cat finding comfort, then you are tumbling in it, mowing down the hill. You floss the taste from your teeth, pinched taste of Novocain, baking soda toothbrush, steam from bath—taste your father's cologne, sliver of soap taste, copper smell of your new woman-taste, sweat on your friend's hand and spit-sister shake. Sugared coffee and fried mozzarella at the gas station taste and blood when you bite your lip taste, boy on the phone and your breath caught in the receiver taste. In the white solid winter when you fall and crack your temple, eyelashes part like hands at prayer's end to alley boys whose fingers over your mouth taste of locker metal, brown paper, rubber, salt, hunger.

Boys

They shone eyes in the hall
between periods.
Boys backlit as new leaves, chins
filling with sprouts, deceived slight tic
of smile for me. It was welcome.
It was mostly unwelcome.
One winnowed his way upstream
abreast of the others: Dan Hook,
who licked his pink lips when
he looked at all of me.
In February, behind Eddie B's,
he slid his tongue in my ear
and breathed. He pulled
my belt loops to make me feel
a malignant thing, risen
unexpected as a tumor.
I felt then my body sprung
from puppet wood.
My bones stuck out
like knots in a trunk. Elbows
jutted like clubs into aisles
between desks. I jerked
stiff through the hall
between periods,
found sap in my underwear.
On walks home I let
the wind blow my black hair
over my face. With each breath
came a faint whistle
only I could hear.

It's Steven Norris

You've forgotten me. I'm a sliver
of your childhood. I watched you
at the food court, walk past the pancake house,
backpack full sagging past your ass,
my little sticky blowpop girl with
fashion patches and a swarm
of starlings landing on the poles above you.
You'll remember my voice
on your personal line. Never mind
how I got it. Your bright, expectant,
innocent hello. I was overjoyed
to tell you all the times I watched you.
Who is this? you said at last, and I didn't answer.
But I should've said this is Steven Norris.
Yours truly, your onlooker. You hung up.
You looked out your third floor window
over all the same-same rooftops.
You put down your blinds. You never told
your parents. A little part of you
must have been flattered.

At Fifteen

with no warning
still dressed
in my school uniform
I turned

fell drunk on Water Street

It was right there
It was the drugs

I dry-wept into the cracked
mirror in an empty warehouse
on South Main
cheeks like my mother's
and father's stern brow

Swam in the filthy
river during the festival

fireworks
domineered
bled and furrowed
from my extremities
Boys roared
and whistled
from cars

Under the inside-out
flag tented over
his bed, the soldier
held my thighs

Smoke treaded August air

I fell and bit
ballast in a train yard

tried to ride blind
hoped for El Paso

I pivoted all too
suddenly
I fell
into the campfire
laughing

like a tree
I cracked
sideways and fell
in the woods and rolled

and I flew over the edge
into a dry crick

Breathless
I looked up

The stars steadied
a meadowlark trilled

I was ready
and coated in silt

On the Younger Self

She was a waitress with a bandana who burned
coffee when the tornado appeared at morning
windows full of motion like child scribble.
In the aftermath, she cried over spilled brick,
carafe still in hand, searched alleyways

for hidden jazz clubs or someone to love
or teach her the Charleston. Found instead
birds with teeth in their beaks pointing
gray wings in accusation. It was difficult

times for the younger self. Two separate
pregnancy tests, eight men in various
beard-lengths, twenty round windows in the capitol
dome watching her scoot around corners. Cleared
her throat before writing a line, looked

to the telephone poles outside her window
for inspiration. Following the storm,
her diaphragm was found embedded in a tree,
displaced zoo beasts rounded up except
the elephant expired directly in the center
of her commute. Miracles zipped past
like dragonflies or gray birds with teeth,
but no one in the passenger seat for her
to elbow and point. At last learning

to swing dance, she felt her limbs arcing
swiftly toward her future, and in the fervent
drum solo, a child somewhere drawing her:
spiral of hair, lines indicating motion.

Falling in Love With the Wrong Man

It isn't all sleeping nude. It isn't playing
the tambourine in a sexy dress
while the audience smolders.
I could care less about the audience. It isn't
shopping for a bungalow with wood floors
shiny as wet skin (though that part
could come later, under normal
circumstances). It's certainly

different than reaching calves out
to swing higher. Because there's so little
effort. A gale can blow you upward if a gale
comes along. Falling in love doesn't always
bring lasting lacerations. Not visibly.
It doesn't always happen in a park.

--

I can tell you like I told the police.
It happens while we're riding
with the top down and it's spring. First,
it beleaguers my hair that surfs wind to brush
against the shoulder of wrong man,
who is driving, (who is a bit gaunt),
whose smile could be first memory,
could be my mother's hem.

My body, feathered through with wires,
receives next installment. The bones move
in foreign ways, arm out the window feels a vortex,
eyes reset in his direction. All motions
are seemingly factory setting.
Primal as lichen, I told them. Feeling along blind.

Wrong man pulls into an empty lot, parks, turns,
winks, oh, still how handsome (though pale),
and exits like a caped villain steps off a precipice.

The bomb has been there all along, snug
between my yellow sandals on the floorboard.
It is disguised as a bag of fertilizer. The zygote

in my womb hiccups in fear (I imagine
that part later). Each movement takes hours
of concentration because my bones are lazy
due to falling in love with the wrong man.
Unbuckle— unlock— open door. I find
an old tree, ubiquitous in this part of town,
and flatten behind it like a lichen seizing the trunk.
The bomb, it turns out, is mostly
fire and confetti. An amateur's explosive. But it attracts
neighborhood people and sirens.

It's too late, I tell them, my arms shaking
with adrenaline, but my cheeks still aglow
with evaporating love. He's gone.

11-B

The outer door squeaks. I force
its echo up the main stair.
Inside your apartment,

bookshelves leer at that portal place
on the carpet. You are gone.
Out the window I see

you carry a sack of laundry
over-the-shoulder in the jaunty
fashion of bearded men.

I eat slowly and wipe
crumbs of stale toast
off my burgeoning baby,

step over the place
on the rug where her two halves
mated, where we tore

my carpet bag and the resolutions
spilled out like entrails.
Rain drums again

and yesterday's puddles
thrum to life. Although I can no longer
see you, I know you are sprinting.

Family Limitation, by Margaret Sanger

My mouth is another womanly opening. I smuggle
a Japanese diaphragm—an obstructive device—
into the chambers of the most fertile
breeder. Confiscated contraceptives wrapped
in cloth and labeled. My mouth is open

like the wound of Christ. My eye
is open, scoped on the menace of pregnancy.
I myself am a mother of three.

Portrait of My Mother as a Young Womb

Portal where daughter,
dawn,   unfurled
to light. Seed claimed
from husk.

Some fourteen years after
my slick departed her squeeze,
I step over her dark shape
in the bathroom. She is
a Gauguin dusk-woman dreaming inside
inaccurate jungle. Her long bereft
womb a broken window.

We become a picnicking
scene, walking into some cusp
of forest, yellow
flower in abundance
in her hair. We're both holding
the handle of a basket we
gathered flowers into,
my hair yellow, but in reality
dye-black shaved
close to skull she forged
herself. We're both holding
the handle of a jug of vodka
and she—goddess,
life, muscle gripped—
yanks it from me
toward her lips.

In a hospital bed, I die and re-enter
fuzzy walls, the red Rothko of
my mother's womb. Water sloshes
each contraction / rejection.
Desperate for the slippery exit—
it's a mouth, my own mouth—I moan
back to clarity and my daughter slips finally
from me—ship from port,

        seed rubbed clean
        from its husk.

A Month After Her Birth

The bed is a cloud and I am afraid
to step off into the cold otherworld,
to take her with me into the vaporous *after.*

I nestle in backwards, pose fetal and pull
her into cocoon of comforter,
to bulge of hot breast,
back to body. I rest.
I bide and tend.

Spring shows in white spurts
through yellowing curtains,
dust stars diving into her breath-stream,
man in green-smelling work boots,
red splash of tulips in his fist
and a new hazel rimming
her muddled irises like moss.

I swaddle us both
and plummet

out to a concrete porch, facing the street.
I see an old friend pass
in a pickup, case of beer clinking in his bed.

Goodbye, I say to him and the shadow-dappled
homes standing casually still
as if no earthquake occurred,
goodbye to infant grass fingering snow.

I breathe the rust of screen door
as it closes me in shadow and squeeze
my new flesh, so long in the making.

Sunday

I reach to yank the chain on your halo
and it's burnt. The water cup
spills in my blanket trails.

The sun is pink
as your Halloween costume,
as your toothpaste spit in the basin.

In my dream, you were chanting
that Louis Prima song:
Oh, yes, we have no bananas!
But we do
and I will.

I told you—be patient! that I will.

The sun floats like an orange bobber
above the placid coffee skim.

I must mush your fruit
very specifically
before I can go there
or to any shore.

Spousal Weaponry

I return home to find you holding
chopsticks and fresh-rolled sushi, only
they're really crochet hooks dipping sharp heads
in apology at my ovaries round as dumplings.

I flap like a stuck moth against the wall.
My accoutrements— hairpins,
        false eyelashes, earrings—
slough off my body like dust. I unfurl my proboscis
to speak but the voice is a pastel feather. Out
        in blue night,

our friends see the shadows on the shades.
Your limbs chop like a marionette. They applaud
because you are a scientist who slips
pills in their drinks. I don't understand

why the wall gulps open like bruised
        esophagus for air—
maybe my skin rubs a fissure apart, but your arm
clamp on my waist wakes me next
        morning. On your breath,
evidence—sawdust. I rise and unroll my plaster tongue.

Walnut Cure

An old lady shakes bobby pins onto my roof.
She throws stones all summer, cracks open air.
Green fingernails, bent torso. Like she
        dances backwards.

Sometimes I dream a black and blue cave.
She sticks her finger in my window and taps me
awake, leaves a verdant bruise. She's begun to intrude.

I stand on the stoop listening late to her wind-pockets
and how she wails to the squirrels to stop
        gnawing her babies.
I'm convinced she's placed a pit in my
        pouch. It becomes

more aware with gulps of sap-water. Inside
        me, the skeleton
of a tree climbs into my throat. She's given me a cure
for dark dreams. I no longer sleep. I grow.

The Witch Baba Yaga

Years lump together where I live
in severance from the wreck of men,
docked inside my shack
in the braided woods,
with my pipe and trance of solitude.

I conjure a façade whenever I sense
a voluptuous maid approaching:
rotting cabin logs take on appearance
of femurs dovetailed into stacks,
child's finger bone for a door handle,
chimney smoke assailing the sky
like rubella rash, ancestral runes
spilt about the ash-gray dirt, and
other convincing intensities.

I take care to furnish my own likeness
with percolating warts, a spider
dangling from ripe mustard hair,
dilate and blood-shoot my eyes,
fork my tongue for good measure
so that when I rasp commands at her
she'll seize on its flicker and scare.

Whole dead years of eating turnip soup
and tearing squirrel thigh from the bone
until a girl, clammy as a priest,
stilts into the dooryard, the tool
of her stepmother's conspiracy. I don
my back hump and rag wool shawl
and stalk out the door to greet her,
poisoned loaf of rye cooling on the sill.

The Cicada Fling

In August the cicada clings –
warlock of the trees, gem
deemed *magicicada.*

He buzzes when held
and crackled in the beak
of the smug jay.

He vibrates the love
hum – live wires
spark in his wings.

The male of the species whistles
in the branches, past lover
at the window, sings

with demand incessant: let me
in, let me in – mouthparts
reek of root juice,

brittle thorax heaves the heart.

Three Night Fever

1.

A black house and a bed.
Tidal pool bed. The first night

I press my palms against the magenta
balloon inflating in my abdomen.

It is polluted with barnacles
and moaning through me.

It ruptures and leaks mustard gas.
My neck stains bilirubin.

2.
My bones turn, betray.
Dried, hardened marshmallows

grind knobs and flake. Don't do it, I say
to the empty and the cats. In snips,

I am aware of myself. In the bathroom
mirror, shrunk except the eyes.

I don't want that, I say to the cats
who are pleased by their freedom.

3.

Going into the night, into fever again,
my muscles take push-cues, synapse pains.

Dreams trying to cross a freeway.
I wake in a stiff soak. Turning, turning,

as if to dough or dirt. The old man
named Steven Norris visits me, leaves a green

ribbon on my sunken hip. The healing is a velvet
tissue. I thank him aloud, find the handle, and lift.

The Day my Husband Left Me for the Desert

I'm going to Buckeye, he said, to dry up.
Slipped his wedding ring off onto
a chain around our daughter's neck.
His chain a twenty-hour drive
rattling, sparking road behind him.
He leans forward, gunning against his hand
rimming a bottleneck. I think there are cacti
sliding up stools beside his car.
When he crosses the border, Texas gravel
shifts like melted ice slivers under his tires.
This is always the way to the desert.
The clouds above beer-head froth.
The rattlesnakes, too, full of venom
and spit. They make a noise like a tip
hits a jar. I am seeing my husband
in a car burnt crisp as a cockroach, scuttling fast
through mountains that snuff the stars.
He is casually smoking, red arm adrift.

Misplace

Nothing is where it should be.
Crickets in the basement, my estranged
husband in the basement
at his mother's suburban home.

There aren't feathers to dust with,
only blunt objects like clocks although
there are no bookends either – spines slip
off the desk and away from my fingers
when I fall asleep on the front stoop.
My children come to carry me indoors
chanting, "light as a feather, stiff as a board."

        Look, I tire.
These tornado sirens drive mother and children
to basement with crickets
at the missing hearth. I thin out.

Dreaming, I try to bandage
all the silvery fish he caught, his hook
            pulling the red membrane
            from their twitching souls.
He's fucking unstoppable with that hook.

But the first aid kit is missing too

and in my dream a tornado did descend
but it was fashioned of paper feathers
that rattled and whispered.
Ah! there they are.

How to Extract the Marriage

Remove the glass coffee table
that deflected words between him
and I until they flitted the room,
smacking windows like flies.
Remove curtains, take down
photos, get out,
away from home.

Go back far
                to Leaf River,
reel again under sharp turbines
in the countryside, drunk a little,
driving back to his mom's from
the cornfield dive.

When I see the stag
with fractals rising on stately head
in ditch weed, —
gesturing in dance to me and speaking —

make him stop the car to look
until he believes me. Take the wheel
and gun the motor until he believes
me. Until buck's blood runs down
the glass if it makes him believe.

After Death: Belle Starr Makes Her Way to Robbers Cave

Shot in the back. For shame. I flew
right out of my sore body, flapping
like an injured crow. I felt
Red Lady gallop within
an inch of my windpipe.
I couldn't cry out.
How the anger pooled.
An oil slick seeping from my wounds.

The assailant escaped—no
face to see under
kerchief. The coward
grunted with heels
to his horse's haunches.
I have an inkling
who he might be.

I'm back now:
transfigured.
I've got a good-sized
plug of revenge
under my tongue.

I figure it will take me
two days heading south
to meet up with the boys
in Latimer County.
What a manhunt we'll launch!—
I have a vision:
coward's blood clouding
Fourche Maline Creek.

Another eye opened
when I flew off Red Lady.
I can see day dimming
and night unleashed, rapidly
bowing in and out
like a child fiddles
with the knob on the sky's lamp.
To be shot in the back—a kind
of liberation.
And nothing to fear
in the deep quiet wood.

Two Ghosts

I erase my ex-husband's name here
because no one knows me. Maybe time
gets away from me. The clock is numberless.
I like to think there's a sudden hush when I coast
through the door in my cloud of
          vanilla. I might be wearing
too much eyeliner. Do I seem earnest?
Colin, the bartender, says a ghost sits in this booth.
When one of the charred men of this bar
takes me in the parking lot—after closing
but before Colin tosses a bucket of ice in the alley—
and drives me to the high woods where
the ghost of Bell Starr watches me bridled,
raped, and tusked through with a hunting knife,
I'll come back to the Wilburton Tap
and sit here in shadowed booth
with the perfect vantage point
to watch Colin's nimble hands
and gray-blue eyes grow old.

Consequences of Removing the Wedding Ring

I no longer snag and the skin underneath
is supple and light. My bare hands unanchored
wobble at the slot that contains
mail-order bees. I release a thousand into
our living room and my daughter
has nightmares of her father, who jumps
off earth and drones away, drunk
on flower scent, holding a cactus needle
like a scabbard. I use sponge-hands gathering
her tears, wring them into my nightly bath.
The water smells like turning milk. I cover
my smile when it tickles across my face.
My fingers grip and release the blessed
pillows that are mine now, mine alone.

Old Story
After "The Butterfly Effect" community mural in Joplin, MO

Bright patches,
vital hues
bandage the wall
of undamaged Dixie Printing Co.
downtown.

The gutting is an old story now.
Cemented in paint,
ash settles
to the right of jagged trees
and grieving
children,

their lines blunt
as wind.

A Monarch shot through
with morning sun
teeters out. In flight,

a phoenix
hovers over
bald ground.

The fiery bird rises, clambers
toward Main, looks around.

The Table

I want to call off the divorce
so I can keep his grandpa's side table.
It is a three-stemmed mushroom
or a waiter's weighted down hand.
I can't imagine a life
in which its upheld tray
no longer proffers my inkwells
and keyholes. I am still in love
with the table. I feel
myself reaching for it
like spooning a phantom in bed.

Eat Something

The food has grown not moldy
but barbed. To eat is to fish
if my tongue were a worm. I can't shield

myself from the fact of geese dying
of fish line and hook obstruction.
Every crumb is a bezoar. I spun

a spoon a million rotations
over the stove, fattened
my husband, patted his rotunda,
delivered too many beers to count. Now

I dole sharp grapes down my gullet.
Food gives you energy.
I peck a crusty bread because
food is life is a thing
they say when they tell me to eat.

The life travels
through goose esophagus,
through body sleeve.
It does reward energy

to resist the want
to quell the rumbling
of my husband's stomach
where he thins across town.

Too Early

My family surgically replaces
my spine with a metal splint. Quick,
outpatient. I am on my feet
at a restaurant, enjoy a frosty beer
with impeccable posture, a doll
on a tool. My father shows,
says it is too early, shame shame
shame this behavior. I don't wanna go

home but there I venture a weed whacker
into mutinous backyard. It's broken, it
won't hum for me. I don't know
how to work metal rod. Fleas joyous leap
a flaccid pool. Power lines
down. Growths yank fence. Even
sunflowers have razored petals.
What happens to a city
reclaimed by nature? I want
back my shorn plateau. I want
back my teacup stack of bones.

On the Forms of Tornadoes

The car door slams on Evelyn's finger. The shock
is a juicy bite cleaved from her apple cheek.
The sucked breath, silence pocket. Then, tornado.

Trees sway into it, their coifs coming
unfurled. Shingles ripple like silver sequins.
Her screams bruise the sky yellow.

Like a maniac, I always run straight to the eye.
Once it took me up like a pile of magnets
so my cells could air out before

pressed back together like a diode.
I feel conducted. I feel like a breeze.
And once when she used her hands

softly by the window stroking dolls,
I saw it through the panes galloping at us
quiet as when a light bulb pops. The tendency

to call it destruction, label it wrath—yes, I
understand. It is also a snapped crayon and a whim
that gathers a thousand feathers to fly.

Sickness and Storm

Croup-cries in the blackout pull me
into the hall lit like horror house
at the carnival, tilted and strobed.
Noises of wind and summer ice
pock the walls and windows.

Evelyn barks vestiges of her
August virus in shadow
while white knives spark
behind her curtains.

I gather her to my chest
in quilts and feel to bed
where the headboard shakes
with each strike like an angry man
must be downstairs heaving
against the front door
with a battering ram.

Snug against my neck,
in breaths like creaking hinge,
Evelyn finds sleep. When electricity
groans on later, I see
her eyelids tranquil
even though my muscles
spasm like a crack
of white in the sky.

Mother-Ghosts

1. Tennessee Town Mother

As a childless young woman, I rented
a bungalow in a *weed-and-seed community.*
The house leaned sideways on its pillars
like an old grave marker.

I raked broken glass in the yard and carried
a camera in my pocket for documenting
my gestures in the home: a painstaking
stew, a row of cacti on the porch railing,

the homage wall to my grandmother,
her grayscale smile finally framed and hung.
Things I deemed important.

I often glimpsed a fast little girl
with blue flower pinned
to her white cardigan
hovering in my kitchen doorway.

I dreamed I tried to grasp her, reached
to hold her trailing black hair
but her shape was a puff of steam
slipping into the vents. I developed

my film. A woman's profile dipped into
nearly every frame, but most clearly
in the photo on my grandmother's wall
where I could see even the strands
of the shadow woman's hair falling
over her shoulder in
reflected glass—leaning
into the room behind me—searching.

2. A Mother's Second-Worst Fear

Now I understand fear. I don't mean
knife-point fear or the wheels of the car
leaving the ground fear. It's an anticipatory
sort of fear that settles on me
like dust, coating thicker the longer
I am a mother. Any number
of horrors can pursue and pin
my child. This is the first,
the worst fear.

       Evelyn's schoolmate was found
riddled with tumors, little death-bulbs
rooting in her spine and the base
of her tender brain. Her body's slow
recession with treatments until she
becomes an elongated infant, hairless,
thin limbs swimming the air.

              The horror—
              her mother I see has shaved her head
              in solidarity with her daughter—
              she wants to be taken instead.

I am certain this is fact.
The mother would rather
the mother be dead.

But that's the second-worst fear:
daughter like a kite when the tether
has snagged and broken away.

That I would die and leave her
follows first fear in dull shadow.
The two thoughts hang around
my neck like a melted chain.

I drive Evelyn to school, drop her
at the entrance with yet another kiss.
How many more kisses do I have.

3. Mother-Rescuer

I don't know this mother, but I know
her story. It frequents me while driving:

She is single, young, pretty with curls
and an oval face quick to beam. Her son is three—
Nicholas who she calls Nicky—
a bright fruit with soft brown hair
sifting into his eyes. Maybe she likes
to mess it in her fingers, then smooth it
into place. She almost certainly does.

Their car in the dark finds the slippery
shoulder and ravine. High forest in California.
A dozen trees splinter sideways
for the pair, but the final
pine insists on its own life,
stands solid as a door
against the flying car
and the mother dies, string
snap. Nicky—stunned, alive.

This is exactly the second-worst fear.

For five days, the boy
swivels to look at his motionless mother, sinks
lower into his seat, till shadows come
and sit on his eyelids. In the night, a driver
sees a naked young woman lying in the road
above the hidden disaster—curly hair, oval face.
Leads police, but then she's gone.

Below, they find her fully clothed, buckled
into instant of her death-place, and her son,
light flicker of life still beating beside her.

4. Image of Myself as a Mother-Ghost

When Evelyn does things like

ask me why I love her in the creamy morning
before I've committed fully to consciousness,

a jerky stick figure inside of me
believes this must be my last day on earth—

the image rises from my sheets. My
daughter can remember how I sleepily

describe my love to her that morning,
later kiss her goodbye at school

and die. Metal to the guardrail—burst
of embolism—other or unknown cause.

Dying is the thing. I then
visit home, leave rings of pinot noir

at the bottoms of glasses at night,
change all the places of bookmarks as if

I'd been up late reading. Pluck lint from Evelyn's
sweater before she walks out. Lightly. Moan

audibly when the sink becomes full of dishes.
Drive an imaginary car to the carpool line,

put on imaginary lipstick, give the other idling parents
a sudden chill at the spine. Slide into Evelyn's

heart-print blankets at night when I'm lonely,
keep trying to grasp her as she drifts into sky.

Campfire

The natural world gathers and expands
like breath. Day slowly opens in pinks
until it's swallowed us in a yellow laugh.
My daughter and I stretch like tongues
from the sleeping bag we shared all night,
                    ripe skin against skin,
and go down to the stream, slip
dirty feet in, so cold and good we gasp.
A heron flies in askance, settles in reeds.

While she watches him preen,
I watch her. My usual shocks commence —
her cheeks plump and smooth as nectarines,
her existence a seed, an unlikely chance.

My own mother liked to camp. I can see
her face in the firelight, the pads of skin
beneath her eyes and the slackening lips.
She let me stay up so late, till stars
were like spilled flour, while she drank
and listened to the radio, unless a man
came along. Then laughs rose higher into
the night and I fell inside her slippery
voice box to sleep. She fell asleep once
with her shoe in the fire. Dark flapping shape
of man in the tent feeling for a jug of water.

Some years later,
her car against the guardrail
burst in a bouquet
of flame. I imagine
even now, she fell asleep
willingly in fire like finding
a warm place in sand.

I am doing this differently. I remember
to pack marshmallows, jacks, butterfly net.
I let her drift asleep in my arms by the fire and no,
I won't fall in. I do prefer cold
opening like a yawn to bring on the day.

After Death: Annie's Mother Considers Signs

The year is 1908, and I am certainly either dead
or having a most thrilling dream. The path

through the wood is coated in young moss
and it is dusk. Pink sun peeks through leaves.

My nine children climb through hickory tops
like imps, each again in bonnets. They laugh

and are fed, with swollen bellies and good color
in the skin. I smile but not wistfully. I'm not here

to gather nuts, but to find my three husbands.
I arrive at a threefold fork and behold

the signposts leading separately to Jacob,
Daniel, and Joseph. My eyes reel to each

arrow, each man's visage erupts midair
like a portrait hung in the parlor. Behind me—

a skirmish, and a hare bolts from a bush, panting.
But, mistaken, I see it's little Phoebe in curls, a gun

perched tight in her hands. I scold her for startling,
but she doesn't hear me at first—instead scopes

three names and shoots them through, raising splinters.
The men with dark chins evaporate. I know not

which path is which. "Are you pleased, Mama?"
Phoebe asks, leans upon her rifle, smiles with missing
       tooth.

Oh Bondage
request to Margaret Sanger

It were my lot, born
with two gunny sacks of eggs
like a slit fish, a hundred babies
waiting in the nether for a day in the sun.
And my husband, turpentine
breath and fistful of my flesh,
conjurer of life. Listless
lives in rough cloth and worms.
Nine, nine, and one on the way.

The doctor said I am a fast breeder.
To abstain. But I am stained
—entered, exited, the milk
pulled endless from my breasts—
on and on, crowd of his making.
Open eyes in the dusk room.
My little bitty stars.

The rich take spoonfuls of caviar—
what it must be like to hold
all those slippery lives in your cheek
and swallow. The rich women
know the secret. How to dam the flow.
I implore you to share. Do you know?

Capitol Postcard

Its thrust rises like our dreams. Here,
depicted in dome restoration like Christ
crowned in scaffold thorns, tiny workers
pinch and rub its pale green cheek
that seems to forever turn away
when you walk it round and round.

Squint now to the distant right:
ours is the gray roof near the hospital.
In stubble garden, blank discs
tied with twine turn and strobe rainbows.
Evelyn comes in from the bus stop,
smelling of burnt snow, her round cheeks

blazing. I tell you I want to pack her
into the hot air balloon with stained glass
pattern that lifts from Lake Shawnee
in the spring. From height, the gray-green

pile of city receding until it's a simple
abrasion forked into abstract farmland.
There's no compositional space
for the sky in this photo.

The Gaze

I woke alone and I was new, my skin
pink and springy. And it became that,
slogging routine, I danced. Danced

whether I cared or not. I was without
a set of eyes watching me, or music. Breakfasting,
danced, and dressing, danced. No one peeped
at me through a window. The sound of the house
sighing in its age. I jutted and thrust to the bus stop,
but people didn't notice. Their eyes thin
as microscope slides. That night,

I collected my skin into an outfit
and went to the night club to dance. There
was a clearing in the middle surrounded by trees.
I stood letting some music flap my hair
about my shoulders. I waved my legs, some,
my hips. My mouth opened and music stole in,
curled up in the center. When I danced,
the animals moved closer, their eyes shining
in the tree line like droplets. When I danced,
the stars watched, the planets, and every
last man swiveled on his bar stool to see
how I opened and lifted my hands.

Letter to Comfort Evelyn

I will never leave you. I will never
cross the state, accelerate away
with music in my hair, road

before me dazzling ribbon, each exit
holding a festival of possible things.

When you pour out of your bed
into dark hall, hands swimming to
magnet of womb, you'll find me.

I'll hear you treading your way like a moth.

Sunflower Postcard

I would visit more often, but if you look between
hollow stems in the field of nodding heads,
you'll notice all that barbed wire. My heart's
bound up in it like a bad tattoo. We're happy, though,
the two of us, stranded. Surrounded by meadows and law.
We're getting to know the place together, like tourists.

Evelyn and I are reading the Wizard of Oz,
but it's given her nightmares of tornadoes.
The dream dictionary says that the tornado
sweeps all in front of it, but after its passage
there is the potential for new life. I also dream
of tornadoes, especially when Evelyn is gone,

across town, breathing in the trundle bed
beside her father. I'm always trying to put her
back inside me so she'll be safe, and we can ride
the tornado across the border to the new life. I am
unafraid. I am actually invincible in dreams.

Friday Night

I see downtown through my face in the mirror.
Young women heave blue plumage into cold air

high on rouged cheek. In my skin's grooves,
a hipbone swing. In black eyes, wobbling moon.

Alley music in the open lips, part and see
inside fluctuating space between bodies

dancing or fumbling on knees. Down
the hall Evelyn sleeps and grows.

Her, too, I see: legs scissor character sheets,
breasts bulb above her slow breaths, teeth

slough out, replace. Soon, a map of fine wrinkles
in her cheeks and rouge like the face of her mother.

I Called the Cops on You

Your house clapped its hips against the street,
sound of tucking or beating
your spouse. Surprise
night club in my alley:
thumping bass thump,
heart of a boy who grew to a man
who beats into crying his wife.

This street is only a red path
at the bottom of a ravine.
People populate the cliff's high walls
in little holes like mouths
shouting out, "I want to be loved," and "I
crave power because I am powerless,"
and hear, too, the little voice
of a child saying simply, "Me."

I called the cops on you. I did.
I watched horrified from a crack
in your closet door,
or grasping the ceiling fan
was how I watched. I saw
everything, officers. It was by his hand

her skull against the wall
like a lollipop. There, the candy
shards. I saw the lights
cut into the street and from my
little perch in the canyon I called
"Me! It was me who did it,
I want so fiercely to matter."

A Front Porch Parable

I went out as the day folded
its golden pancake into the horizon,
hungry for the air apart
from the kind controlled by a dial,
the kind of air that costs.

A fox lives under my porch,
breathing the humid puff
summer exhales. I stood out front,
looked at clouds, and as I often do,
imagined horses and buggies in place of cars.

A cockroach fell into my hair
from the rotten boards.
When I shook it off it slithered
away, wore a brown rayon suit jacket
and carried photographs of semi-nude women
using a lavatory, which it had taken
through a roach's peep hole.

Insect mascot of the poor. In the clouds
I saw a troupe of parasites
descending on wings and chutes.
What I meant to say all along is

I stepped out on the veranda
wearing a Nile scarab in my crown.
A parade of buggies streamed through the street.
I have a pet fox. Her name is Maxine.

Asylum Postcard

Architecture gesture of late nineteenth century—
you can see the Viennese influence, nothing lush
in its spires and wings, but still, understated beauty

that fell to the wrecking ball this spring. We strode up
where the dust rolled like a tsunami through our streets
and saw two foxes fleeing. Evelyn cried

that they ruined her castle. I wonder if she'll remember
when she's older how blonde bricks rained for days
like a slow motion tornado. In the picture you see

a smudge on high window that could be a face,
orderly pausing from initialing reports to gaze
at the grounds. I told Evelyn how they held dances

for the inmates in the ballroom but left off
darker things. When she's older maybe I'll tell her
about you and I clamoring through the abandoned

asylum, tempting ghosts. Maybe they snuffed
our little ember that night. My younger self is still
there, surviving brickfall, dust flood, wandering

the bald swath left behind when bulldozers scraped it away.

Letter to the Lost Father

It takes a man to make a son.
I am the woman to raise him—
hazy shape in the night when he calls.
The soft skull with its feathered whorl

is fatherless. Does it matter.
For now, I am the finger
he is wrapped around. He

gestured vaguely inside me,
little limpid flag. Was it a signal
that brought you close to share
my breath so briefly? You

are gone. I barely knew
the man it took to make
a rooting mouth, an empty
belly I'll fill tonight, tomorrow,

and further. How far-
reaching your one short gasp.
How firmly he
grasps my finger.

Morning Storm

Come light I find the whole house churned adrift through
       flood water, raising a wake, roaring like a monster
       truck,

and glimpse my children—dervishes traveling city streets
       on cracked garbage can lids

while the neighbors look on from the safety of duck-yellow
       rafts tethered to poles, clucking disapproval.

My lone tree, the walnut so far only good for flinging
       stones at slouched gutter, turns and plucks me
       from bed, abrades my cheek, squelches its roots
       deeper as my home dips west.
The porch swing waves like a broken arm. Thunder makes
       the noise of a sucking drain and God's hand
       overhead like the shadow of a falling bird

reaches to wipe the steam from the tallest building
       downtown.

The Bird Woman

A woman in orbs of latex—I've seen her
bursting from her screen door to throw molded
hunks of cheese and tortilla discs to the crows,
turtle doves, and starlings. Drugs,
I think, or instability. Unlike me, she
has a man, tall and silent, who darkens
the back door while she suns herself
on a rubber recliner. The birds
ladder the chain link fence with bits
of food in their sharp beaks, cast
fluttering shadows on her white, white skin.
She's in her place, her menagerie. I am
a mousy woman with wide eyes gathering
the mail, herding my children to the door,
watering the back porch plants. But I too
have things to discard, rotten bits to cast out
my door. And a certain pleasure, I can see,
may be derived from watching such things
plucked to shreds, gobbled, and gone.

Backyard

It's loud as a rainforest.
Starlings squawk
in redbud trees. The wind
convinces leaves to show
their pale undersides,
to shimmy.

The girl pushes dandelion mop heads
into a fallen leaf to make a token for me
and the boy stops scaring robins
to stare at sky. A storm

dressed in evening pink
unfurls and grows,
bouquet stewed in the south.

Nearly May, various seeds
flit and spray
through air, fitful to cling. Before

I know what has happened,
the whole of it has silenced.

Above my head a dark sight
thrums and swoops, careens
fast to the blunt flatness
of fence post. Fallen starling,

parted beak, gasp of dread,
glint-wing broken open
in sinister cape. I cup
its gloss in my palm.

The children fret and coo as I carry the bird
to a canopied place, wish it peace,
and bow away from its pointing eye.

The storm's outskirt arrives
in black overhead. The wind
grips my face, tells me to get inside.

Fleas and Biting Things

Typical, it began with the dog.
They slipped beneath her white fur
like skinny dippers entering a reservoir.

Then they teemed at my ankles, bit
my tattoos, making the old scrawl puff
cartoonish. I caught one and pressed to kill,

but my fingers were train wheels on the rail.
It nestled into my fingerprint grooves.
Released, the flat speck gathered springs and flung.

--

Children who cohabit with fleas wake in the night
pleading for medicine. Their hidden-most skin is a feast.
Their mother is a slow giant with fumbling hands.

Biting things must be the cause of their sunken eyes,
their legs restless in the lively sheets.
I tie their laces in a black hailstorm, send them to school.

--

Typically, each family has a battle with the invisible.
Ours was scabies. Magma under the skin,
turning my sister and I into fiends with teeth

for gnawing our own wrists. Our sins
bubbled like proofing yeast. We waded
into the foam, moaning,

raw meat walking—
consumed, a pilgrimage of nothing-beings rippling
in waves over lush muscles to the anthills of our hearts.

Two bony girls lay side-by-side in a tepid bath,
oatmeal grit collecting in ear canals, eyelashes, navels.
They chose us because we were already weak.

--

The children are getting that look about them:
like deer in January, their legs knobby, eyes wet,
the fuzz of their skin smelling of wood smoke.

I wish I could rage like in dreams—punch the snout of a puma,
wring a snake, bite the neck of a black bear. Instead,
I pat and caress ointment into the pores,

release a plume of fairy smoke,
mercifully put the enemy to sleep, uncoil
springs, wrap them in a smother—

all black biting things drop mid-air, seized.
We're left with pocked ankles and we sleep heavy
as if nothing unseen eyes the ripe land of rising skin.

Co-Sleep

The children nearly strangers
scale the bed affix feelers
to my hips
breathe there dream I am
mean I mistake
them for opening wings
each a lengthening
bundle house

There was a year
I had no money
and two golden babies
who I fed with
milk thread through my skin—
tincture of garden dirt
on white pumping tongues

in this same bed
We wrench sheets away
from each other
turning mills churn breath
flap the shades
separate and I
fall out of the bed—
bones splashing the night—
blinking pain—and stay awake
go where I can keep
the light lit and sleep is for
children who grow

Nostalgia #4

Mustard-yellow petals unfurled
across the surface where an ill-fated love bloomed.
Let's say it was the love of my parents. It was
slightly out of focus. A broken zipper,
in the picture, belonged to my father. Outside, perhaps,

a sidewalk belongs to my child mother. She is younger, where
I will never be again. Sucking a popsicle. Her breasts
are yet hard knots. A walnut tree with fisty roots upturns
a section of her sidewalk. I cannot see the sidewalk

in this photograph because of the wool curtains
with an ochre apple print. I am eager to smell the tree sap
out-liming the Lava soap of father's farmer hands
but not yet smothering my mother's light
berry popsicle scent. Get this—the sun was there, too.
This very same sun. The sidewalk is gone, and gone
the moment before the picture, when he led her
away from her claim of sidewalk

with his lime-scalded hands,
into the house, to the floral table
and onto his lap for the picture—see,
she is the smiling child.

Nostalgia #5

I went three days with no nostalgia.
In the evening of the first day,
I took a sleeping pill and pulled the lid
off a sewer cap beneath my bed.
The tunnels meant nothing
without the headlamp between
my eyes. By light I mean emotion.
It was three days of darkness.

By day I experienced events in real time
I knew I would later want to pine for.
Simple whispers, like my leisurely hand
out the car window after a rain and,
out of curiosity, kissing my own cold knee.
I cooked a good meal, felt grateful to myself.
I took no pictures. Don't ever look back.
A traveling carnival put down stakes in our town
but my longing would be suffocation
in a place like that. I would feel, at once,
all the tongues of boy lovers
jammed into my grape-flavored
mouth. I would feel the latch of my throat
open quick to laughter by a manic squad
of girls who were, for a night, my friends.

I want none of these flowers bursting
in my eyelids. I'll never go there again.

The Rental

I stroke the walls
with a brush souped in iodine.
I stroke them, look for an opening

for a needle or finger
so I can reach out
and find what I need.

A boy sends me a text:
"Why don't you come
watch this redbox movie w/ me"

The wall doesn't open.
"Nah" I peck back.
I peck at the walls.

I go outside and get into
my car. It jumps alive at my touch.
All down the street, twinkles

of home-love, and above
the earth's warm bread body,
a blue nightgown opens and billows.

I look for an opening
in the windshield. A place to slip
a key or thermometer.

I wonder what movie
and sense an opening
in my skin. I'm the place

he moved out of last week,
turned the keys in, shut the door
with a last little suck of air.

The Rental

Little windows, a face peers from a square.
Tiny house that accordions inward. Shotgun
shack. Blue gutters and trim. Dirty windows,
dirty me. Leaves everywhere, they're in

my lungs. And acorns brimming the thresholds.
I swish mouse droppings into the dustpan.
Sop water leaks. Glide through
the monthly money. Feel the money heat.

Peering from the square, I note the brambles.
I can unlock the door and fall inside, tripped
by wires slithered from walls. I can
go to the bath and climb inside. It is colder
at night when the dark begins to touch

the rooftop. It is night and I am waiting
for you to arrive. I've left the front door open.
A square of light on the street.

Ashley

Before any of this, —
brush through hair in the morning, tin for keys, tin
for barrettes, assortment of purses and closets to clean,
physical, carpool, newsletter, tips for fuss-free dinner,

                — there was Ashley and I hot-basking
at the space heater on Lincoln Street in fingerless gloves

first Kansas winter. I mistook
the caraway colored place for the south.

Ice storm roofs, ice storm river,
lines of ice draped across the yard
falling like whips. City dark, comatose
like we'd all pricked our fingers on capitol's spindle.

Ashley and I clipped open cans with church keys
and ate, went to shows, stole, danced grinning,
rode in the backseat with the amber
capitol flashing us like lighthouse.

            Back home our boots at the door
stiff as bark and rags stuffed in jambs and sills
like Ashley's dustbowl ancestors.

She and I —
slept in separate rooms connected
through a transom tunnel, function of ear.
At night, gasps like she drowned but
no sound from her man. Mine slept beside me
curled like frozen locust pod, waiting
to crumble in my fist. And he did, sifted away.

        The other day —
Ashley and I get tipsy at a too-nice place,
laugh and billow back to the car for a shared stale
cigarette dug from dash. I know you, we say.
How strange to know you now. Ashley's white-blue
eyes lighten and dart. It's cold. Winter's coming.

Press

I put the house key on the track.
I put the steel wedding band
onto the track with the train
eating closer to the bend.
I placed the baby's jumpsuit there
who is no longer a baby, but a child.
I put down her wiggled-out teeth. With care,
I arranged an empty collar on the track.
I took out the bitten place on my thigh
and pressed that to the track with the train
chewing closer. I put a deed. I put
a certificate. A roll of bloodied gauze.
I unwrapped a man who still smelled
of my perfume and roped him to the track.
The trembling track. I cupped my hands
to catch the nails, tacks, and hinges
spilling from my eyes and put them
right under the opening maw.
I turned my back to the beckoning shriek
and went down the hill.

I Have Decided

I have decided to hold both of my children in one hand like worry balls and thrust them high above people milling in a gallery at the Nelson, where I would go before I had children to push and pull myself at a painting as if pulling gum from my shoe. I will hold them above the crowd, have one hand free to thrash us to the exit. Have one hand free to wipe my brow. One hand to test the wind's direction. One to place in the offered hands of a man, someone with bear hands who can fold mine into a crane. He must be satisfied with just the one hand. If it turns out he is unsatisfied with just the one hand, I will sit down and write this poem.

At Thirty

after Amy Fleury

I danced in my kitchen
with YouTube, strobe lights, my
two children. I cracked

the back door to air out the fog,
drank wine long into night
after my true loves had fallen

asleep pressed by the television's blue
hand. I woke that year coughing
up fear. I thinned out and

took the children often to the frog pond
in the forest, contemplated
its skin of scum: what would it feel

like in my mouth? Grit, calm,
a tongue? Dreamed the bejeweled
frogs fetched to my thighs like ivy and

any lover I ever had—bears
glimpsed in the woods, scaring
my children pale and white-haired.

I slept in trickles. Woke
with the fear clot
loose in my throat.

I laughed it out. I laughed
and sang in the kitchen
later in life, in the middle

of the room, swinging my arms,
jumping, hair in my eyes—this body
moving proof it's alive.

Ashley Laird, *For Leah*. Pencil on paper. 2009.

103

Leah Sewell is the author of *Mother-Ghosts* and *Birth in Storm* and her work has appeared in *Midwestern Gothic, burntdistrict, [PANK], Bridge Eight* and elsewhere. She's the founder of *Microburst*, the Andy Warhol Foundation-supported zine of art, literature and politics. She's an Arty Award recipient for excellence in literary arts, an MFA grad of the University of Nebraska, a graphic artist, editor, cook, and mother to two wily youths. Her website is leahsewell.com.

www.ingramcontent.com/pod-product-compliance
Lightning Source LLC
Chambersburg PA
CBHW051734040426
42447CB00008B/1131